CHEMISTRY EXPLAINED

# MOLECULES & CHEMICAL REACTIONS

by
Janet Bingham

Minneapolis, Minnesota

**Credits**

Cover and title page, © Ezume Images/Adobe Stock Images; 3, © Who is Danny/Adobe Stock Images; 4T, © seqoya/Adobe Stock Images; 4B, © Gino Santa Maria/Adobe Stock Images; 4–5, © Gorodenkoff/Adobe Stock Images; 5B, © viktoriya89/Adobe Stock Images; 6T, © anchalee thaweeboon/Shutterstock; 6B, © Atlantist Studio/Shutterstock; 6–7, © Bedrin/Shutterstock; 7T, © zizou7/Shutterstock; 7B, © MRC Laboratory of Molecular Biology/Wikimedia Commons; 8T, © Charles Shapiro/Shutterstock; 8M, © Net Vector/Shutterstock; 8B, © MRC Laboratory of Molecular Biology/Wikimedia Commons; 8–9, © Rings and jewelery/Alamy Stock Photo; 10T, © 2DAssets/Shutterstock and © trgrowth/Shutterstock; 10B, © Science Source/Science Photo Library; 10–11, © Martyn F. Chillmaid/Science Photo Library; 11T, © Turtle Rock Scientific/Science Photo Library; 12T, © Kedar Vision/Shutterstock; 12M, © peterschreiber.media/Shutterstock; 12B, © Sansanorth/Shutterstock; 12–13, © Idutko/Shutterstock; 13M, © MarcelClemens/Shutterstock; 13B, © MRC Laboratory of Molecular Biology/Wikimedia Commons; 14T, © LoopAll/Shutterstock; 14B, © zizou7/Shutterstock; 14–15, © imageBROKER/Alamy Stock Photo; 15B, © Harvard University/Wikimedia Commons; 16T, © nguyen thi phuong dieu/Shutterstock; 16M, © Stephen Mcsweeny/Shutterstock; 16B, © Maria Symchych/Shutterstock; 16–17, © Halfpoint/Shutterstock; 17TL, © Bearport Publishing; 18T, © Stivog/Shutterstock; 18B, © Eric Hood/Adobe Stock Images; 18–19, © VH-studio/Shutterstock; 19B, © Universal History Archive / UIG/Science Photo Library; 20T, © Baiphai Bamboo/Shutterstock; 20B, © pio3/Shutterstock; 20–21, © 2011 Sara Dawn Johnson/Getty Images; 22T, © PA Images/Alamy Stock Photo; 22B, © Net Vector/Shutterstock; 22–23, © YouraPechkin/Shutterstock; 23T, © Hecos/Shutterstock; 23B, © MRC Laboratory of Molecular Biology/Wikimedia Commons; 24T, © Andy Dean Photography/Shutterstock; 24B, © successo images/Shutterstock; 24–25, © VasiliyBudarin/Shutterstock; 25B, © Bearport Publishing; 26T, © Nobeastsofierce/Science Photo Library; 26B, © MRC Laboratory of Molecular Biology/Wikimedia Commons; 26–27, © Peter Mayer 67/Shutterstock; 27T, © Curioso.Photography/Shutterstock; 28M, © Chaleephoto/Shutterstock; 28B, © MRC Laboratory of Molecular Biology/Wikimedia Commons; 28–29, © Engineer studio/Shutterstock; 29T, © Chaleephoto/Shutterstock; 30B, © trgrowth/Shutterstock; 30–31, © Andrew Lambert Photography/Science Photo Library; 31T, © Pictorial Press Ltd/Alamy Stock Photo; 32M, © Sergey Merkulov/Shutterstock; 32B, © Harvard University/Shutterstock; 32–33, © Robert Kneschke/Shutterstock; 33T, © ggw/Shutterstock; 34T, © Egoreichenkov Evgenii/Shutterstock; 34B, © buteo/Shutterstock; 34–35, © SAKKMESTERKE/Science Photo Library; 35T, © OSweetNature/Shutterstock; 35B, © Science History Institute/Wikimedia Commons; 36M, © Dorling Kindersley Ltd/Alamy Stock Photo; 36B, © Harvard University/Wikimedia Commons; 36–37, © William Perugini/Shutterstock; 37T, © Anatoly Foto/Shutterstock; 38T, © Mark Agnor/Shutterstock; 38M, © WillemijnB/Shutterstock; 38B, © Science History Institute/Wikimedia Commons; 38–39, © H. Mark Weidman Photography/Alamy Stock Photo; 39T, © Sokor Space/Shutterstock; 40T, © Zigres/Shutterstock; 40B, © Ulianenko Dmitrii/Shutterstock; 40–41, © sebra/Shutterstock; 41TL, © Science History Institute/Wikimedia Commons; 41MR, © EYE OF SCIENCE/Science Photo Library; 42M, © Halfpoint/Adobe Stock Images; 42B, © clemMTravel/Adobe Stock Images; 42–43, © NanTua/Adobe Stock Images; 43B, © Markus Mainka/Adobe Stock Images; 44B, © Gorodenkoff/Adobe Stock Images;45T, © peterschreiber.media/Shutterstock; 45B, © Bedrin/Shutterstock; 47B, © Sakkmesterke/Science Photo Library

**Bearport Publishing Company Product Development Team**

Publisher: Jen Jenson; Director of Product Development: Spencer Brinker; Editorial Director: Allison Juda; Editor: Cole Nelson; Editor: Tiana Tran; Production Editor: Naomi Reich; Art Director: Kim Jones; Designer: Kayla Eggert; Designer: Steve Scheluchin; Production Specialist: Owen Hamlin

**Statement on Usage of Generative Artificial Intelligence**

Bearport Publishing remains committed to publishing high-quality nonfiction books. Therefore, we restrict the use of generative AI to ensure accuracy of all text and visual components pertaining to a book's subject. See BearportPublishing.com for details.

Library of Congress Cataloging-in-Publication Data is available at www.loc.gov or upon request from the publisher.

ISBN: 979-8-89577-499-1 (hardcover)
ISBN: 979-8-89577-541-7 (paperback)
ISBN: 979-8-89577-507-3 (ebook)

© 2026 Arcturus Holdings Limited. This edition is published by arrangement with Arcturus Publishing Limited.

North American adaptations © 2026 Bearport Publishing Company. All rights reserved. No part of this publication may be reproduced in whole or in part, stored in any retrieval system, or transmitted in any form or by any means, electronic, mechanical, photocopying, recording, or otherwise, without written permission from the publisher. Bearport Publishing is a division of FlutterBee Education Group.

For more information, write to Bearport Publishing, 3500 American Blvd W, Suite 150, Bloomington, MN 55431.

# Contents

Small but Powerful . . . . . . . . . . . . . . . . . . . . . . 4

Atomic Structure . . . . . . . . . . . . . . . . . . . . . . 6

Elements . . . . . . . . . . . . . . . . . . . . . . . . 8

Energy Shells . . . . . . . . . . . . . . . . . . . . . . . 10

Molecules . . . . . . . . . . . . . . . . . . . . . . . 12

Compounds . . . . . . . . . . . . . . . . . . . . . . 14

Important Properties . . . . . . . . . . . . . . . . . 16

Conductors and Insulators . . . . . . . . . . . . . 18

Viscosity Oddities . . . . . . . . . . . . . . . . . . 20

Changing States . . . . . . . . . . . . . . . . . . . 22

Mixtures and Solutions . . . . . . . . . . . . . . . 24

Diffusion and Brownian Motion . . . . . . . . . . 26

Separating Solids from Mixtures . . . . . . . . 28

Separating Solutions . . . . . . . . . . . . . . . . 30

Reactions . . . . . . . . . . . . . . . . . . . . . . . . 32

Radioactivity . . . . . . . . . . . . . . . . . . . . . . 34

Reversible and Irreversible Changes . . . . . . 36

Exothermic and Endothermic Reactions . . . 38

Speeding Up Reactions . . . . . . . . . . . . . . . 40

Molecules Make the World . . . . . . . . . . . . . 42

Review and Reflect . . . . . . . . . . . . . . . . . . 44

Glossary . . . . . . . . . . . . . . . . . . . . . . . . . 46

Read More . . . . . . . . . . . . . . . . . . . . . . . . 47

Learn More Online . . . . . . . . . . . . . . . . . . . 47

Index . . . . . . . . . . . . . . . . . . . . . . . . . . . 48

# Small but Powerful

All of the matter in the universe is made up of tiny molecules. These molecules are so small that they cannot be seen without a powerful microscope, but they can still be broken up into still smaller atoms. Some molecules are made of a single type of atom, but many of the most useful molecules contain two or more different types of atoms bonded together.

## Everyday Reactions

When molecules react, they form or break bonds and create new substances in the process. Chemical reactions are happening around us all the time. For example, an apple reacts to the oxygen in the air when it is sliced. Molecules in the fruit combine and react with amino acids to create a brown pigment.

Chemicals called quinones react with amino acids in apples to create the brown pigment melanin.

## Stunning Transformations

Some chemical reactions can produce very dramatic effects. Fireworks use reactions that create light, heat, and even sound. When a fuel in a firework, such as charcoal, reacts with a type of chemical called an oxidizer, they bond together. This reaction creates a lot of energy and gas, resulting in spectacular explosions.

## Conserving Mass

Every chemical reaction follows certain universal laws. One such law is the law of conservation of mass, which states that mass is neither created nor destroyed in a reaction. We can see this when burning a candle. The candle becomes smaller, but that mass of the missing wax is not lost. It's just changed into gases and ash.

# Atomic Structure

All matter in the universe is made of tiny atoms. Atoms contain the even smaller subatomic particles protons, neutrons, and electrons. The number of these subatomic particles determines the properties of the atom. The variety of atomic structure gives us the 118 elements we know today.

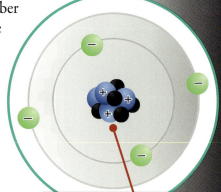

Beryllium has atomic number 4. Its nucleus has four protons (light blue) and five neutrons (dark blue). Four electrons (green) are arranged in two surrounding energy shells.

## The Atomic Nucleus

The nucleus in the middle of an atom is made up of protons and neutrons. These subatomic particles are packed together into a cluster that is 2,000 times heavier than the electrons surrounding the nucleus. An element's atoms all have the same number of protons. This is its atomic number.

## Electrons

Outside of the nucleus, an atom is mostly empty space. Electrons—subatomic particles with a negative charge—whiz around in energy shells or layers surrounding the nucleus. Each shell is a layer that can hold a set number of electrons, so atoms with more electrons have more shells. The equal and opposite charges of the protons and electrons in an atom attract each other, creating an electromagnetic force that holds atoms together. On the whole, atoms have the same number of electrons as protons, giving the particles no charge.

Energy shells are stacked inside one another like Russian dolls. But the shells are not solid. Only electromagnetic attraction holds the electrons close to the nucleus.

**DID YOU KNOW?** Protons and neutrons contain even tinier particles called quarks and gluons. Scientists know of 36 subatomic particles so far!

**Carbon 12**
6 Protons
6 Neutrons
6 Electrons

**Carbon 13**
6 Protons
7 Neutrons
6 Electrons

**Carbon 14**
6 Protons
8 Neutrons
6 Electrons

The total number of protons and neutrons in the nucleus is the atom's mass number.

Isotopes are forms of an element with different numbers of neutrons. A normal carbon atom—Carbon 12—has a nucleus with six neutrons, but other isotopes have seven or eight.

The first energy shell is closest to the nucleus. It can contain up to two electrons.

As the shells fill up with electrons, more shells are added. The heaviest atoms have more than 100 electrons in 7 shells.

Bigger atoms have more shells, farther out from the nucleus. The second and third shells can contain up to eight electrons each.

### Joseph John Thomson
### 1856–1940

English physicist J. J. Thomson discovered the electron in 1897. His experiments showed that cathode rays, or the rays seen when electricity flows through gases at low pressure, were streams of particles with much less mass than atoms themselves. We now call these particles electrons. He was awarded the Nobel Prize in Physics in 1906.

**HALL OF FAME**

# Elements

The atoms of different elements have different numbers of protons, neutrons, and electrons. The properties of an element, or the way it looks and behaves, are due to the number of each subatomic particle in its atoms.

Air is a mixture of gases, including the elements nitrogen, oxygen, and argon. The element in a blimp, helium, is a gas that is lighter than air, so it floats in the sky.

### Names and Numbers

We know of 118 elements. Around 90 are found naturally, while the rest are synthetic, or made by scientists. Synthetic elements usually have many protons, making them unstable and prompting them to decay quickly into elements with fewer protons. Each element is identified by its atomic number, or the number of protons inside one atom's nucleus. And every element is also given a name and a symbol of one or two letters. For example, hydrogen has the symbol H, and lead has the symbol Pb.

## All Our Resources

At room temperature, only two elements are liquids—mercury and bromine. Eleven are gases. The rest are solids, with most of these being metals. Some, such as gold, occur naturally in a pure form. However, most elements are found in impure forms as compounds, or mixtures, with other elements. Elements and their compounds make up the minerals and rocks of Earth's crust.

Silicon oxide, a compound of oxygen and silicon, makes up most of Earth's crust as rocks or sand. Aluminum, iron, and calcium are the next three most common elements in the crust.

**HALL OF FAME**

### Ida Noddack, née Tacke
#### 1896–1978

The element rhenium was first isolated in 1925 in Germany by Ida Tacke, Otto Berg, and Walter Noddack—Ida's future husband. This element has a very high melting point and is now used in aircraft engines. Ida was also the first to suggest that atoms bombarded by neutrons might split into smaller atoms through nuclear fission. Four years later, this was shown to be possible.

Copper is a trace element, meaning there is a tiny amount in your body that keeps you healthy.

We often see gold, silver, and copper made into decorative items, but these metallic elements have many more uses.

Silver is an excellent conductor, or carrier, of heat and electricity. It reflects light effectively as well and is used in mirrors and solar panels.

Gold is very unreactive. It does not react with air and so does not tarnish, or lose its shine. It also conducts electricity well. Because of this, gold is used in many electronic devices.

**DID YOU KNOW?** The most recently discovered element, tennessine, was made in a laboratory in 2010.

9

# Energy Shells

Each atom has energy shells that can hold up to a certain number of electrons. The first and innermost shell can hold two electrons. Each shell farther out from the nucleus can hold more electrons. Shells are most stable when they hold the maximum number of electrons. Stable elements are less reactive, meaning they do not interact with other atoms as much as unstable elements.

## Outer Shell Electrons

Elements with the same number of electrons in their outer energy shell behave in similar ways. This is true even if the elements have different numbers of energy shells. For example, lithium has two energy shells, sodium has three, and francium has seven shells. But each of these elements has an outermost shell with just one solitary electron. Since they are all ready to give up their solitary electron, these elements are very reactive.

Alkali metals all have one electron in their outermost energy shells. They are used in many different industries.

- Li (Lithium) — Cell phone batteries
- Na (Sodium) — Salt
- K (Potassium) — Fertilizer
- Rb (Rubidium) — Fireworks
- Cs (Cesium) — Atomic clocks
- Fr (Francium) — Radioactive materials

**HALL OF FAME**

### Marguerite Catherine Perey
### 1909–1975

In 1939, francium became the last naturally occurring element to be discovered. It was the only element to be discovered solely by a woman. Marguerite Catherine Perey was separating radioactive elements when she found one that fit the gap at atomic number 87 in Mendeleev's periodic table. She named it francium after her home country, France.

10

## Alkali Metals

The alkali metals are the elements lithium, sodium, potassium, rubidium, and cesium, plus radioactive francium. These shiny metals are soft enough to cut with a knife. They all react readily with other chemicals, but the ones with more energy shells are more reactive than those with fewer. These elements react with cold water by releasing heat in an exothermic reaction. When combined with some nonmetals, they form white crystalline salts that dissolve easily in liquids. For example, sodium reacts with chlorine to form sodium chloride, also known as table salt.

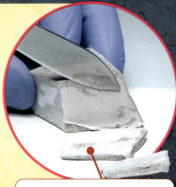

Alkali metals react with oxygen in the air to make metal oxides. The bright, newly cut surface of sodium tarnishes in moments. Potassium reacts even faster!

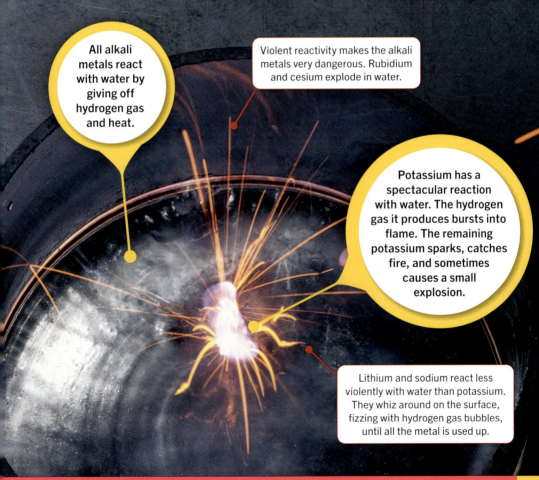

All alkali metals react with water by giving off hydrogen gas and heat.

Violent reactivity makes the alkali metals very dangerous. Rubidium and cesium explode in water.

Potassium has a spectacular reaction with water. The hydrogen gas it produces bursts into flame. The remaining potassium sparks, catches fire, and sometimes causes a small explosion.

Lithium and sodium react less violently with water than potassium. They whiz around on the surface, fizzing with hydrogen gas bubbles, until all the metal is used up.

**DID YOU KNOW?** Cesium atomic clocks are the most accurate clocks in the world, losing or gaining just one second every 1,400,000 years!

# Molecules

Atoms like to stick together! Only a few—those that make up the noble gases—keep to themselves. Most atoms bond with other atoms to make molecules. Molecules can be composed of only a couple of atoms, or they can be giant molecular structures. A crystal is a structure in which the atoms or molecules join up in a regular, repeating pattern.

Diamond is the hardest natural substance on Earth. Many of these crystals are made into jewelry, but diamonds are also used in industrial tools.

Hydrogen is a diatomic element. By pairing up and sharing their electrons to make a bond, two hydrogen atoms make a stable, homonuclear molecule.

## Diatomic Molecules

There are two atoms in diatomic molecules. If the atoms are identical, the molecule is homonuclear. Elements with atoms that pair up in this way are diatomic elements. The bond is made by sharing electrons, which fill up both atoms' energy shells. A hydrogen atom has one electron, but its shell can hold two—so two hydrogen atoms share their two electrons.

## Allotropes

The crystals of some elements are simple. They contain only one kind of atom. Yet they can be surprising. Their atoms join together in different ways to make different allotropes. Two allotropes of carbon are diamond and graphite. Diamond and graphite have different properties because of the ways their atoms are arranged.

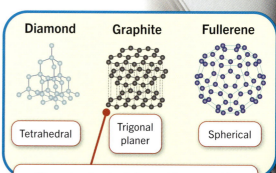

Diamond — Tetrahedral

Graphite — Trigonal planer

Fullerene — Spherical

The molecular sheets in graphite are weakly bonded, so graphite is softer than diamond, which has strong bonds in all directions. Another allotrope—fullerene—has atoms in a sphere.

**12**   **DID YOU KNOW?** The largest uncut diamond ever found weighed more than 1 pound (0.45 kg). It was cut into more than 100 gemstones.

A pencil drawing is made of graphite. Both graphite and diamond are giant molecular structures of carbon.

Soft graphite is used in pencils because its molecules easily slide over one another and rub off on the paper, leaving a mark behind.

Crystals of the element sulfur can be shaped as four-sided pyramids or as long needles. These different forms are allotropes.

### Rosalind Franklin
#### 1920–1958

British scientist Rosalind Franklin studied molecules using X-ray crystallography. She helped to discover the double helix structure of deoxyribonucleic acid (DNA). She also made important discoveries about the structure of viruses, as well as about the different forms of carbon in coal and graphite. Her work on carbon paved the way for the development of useful carbon fiber technologies.

**HALL OF FAME**

# Compounds

Compounds are molecules with more than one kind of atom. They are made when the atoms of different elements react and bond together. The different chemicals in a compound can be separated only by a chemical change that breaks their bonds.

## Compound Properties

No atoms are lost when chemicals react. This means the total chemicals at the start and end of a reaction—the reactants and the products—contain the same atoms in different combinations. The products have new properties, meaning they look and behave differently from the reactants. When you drink water, you are drinking a liquid compound of the gases hydrogen and oxygen. When you lick salt, you are eating a compound of the gas chlorine and the metal sodium.

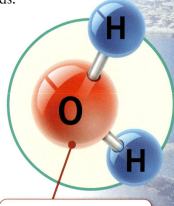

Chemicals have more than one name. A water molecule has two hydrogen atoms and one oxygen atom, so it is also called dihydrogen oxide.

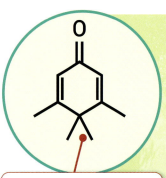

The structural chemical formula of 3,4,4,5-tetramethyl-2,5-cyclohexadien-1-one looks a bit like a penguin. The chemical's common name is penguinone.

## Names and Formulas

Some compounds contain many elements and have complicated names to describe them. Luckily, scientists give chemicals simpler common names as well. They also have a clever, short way of describing compounds through chemical formulas. Every element has a symbol of one or two letters, and these make up the chemical formulas of all possible compounds. The formula for water is $H_2O$, which shows that the molecule has two hydrogen atoms and one oxygen atom. Chemists also use diagrams called structural chemical formulas to show the links between atoms.

**DID YOU KNOW?** Made in 2014, the largest molecule, PG5, contains 17 million atoms of carbon, nitrogen, and oxygen.

The terraces of Pamukkale in Turkey are a natural wonder formed by underground thermal springs rising to Earth's surface.

The beautiful white limestone pools are made out of calcium carbonate ($CaCO_3$), a compound of calcium, carbon, and oxygen that is carried up in water from underground.

Calcium carbonate is dissolved in liquid water underground. When the water cools at the surface, the $CaCO_3$ turns back into a solid.

The process of a dissolved chemical leaving the solution and becoming solid is called precipitation.

### Marie-Anne Lavoisier
### 1758–1836

Marie-Anne Lavoisier and her husband Antoine had a laboratory at their home in Paris, where they invited other scientists to watch and debate their experiments. As Antoine's coworker, illustrator, translator, and assistant, Marie-Anne Lavoisier was essential to their shared research. Among other things, the couple identified oxygen and showed that it reacts with other elements to make compounds.

**HALL OF FAME**

# Important Properties

Every element and compound has unique properties because of its structure. We build with materials that have properties that make them fit for certain jobs. Hardness, roughness, flexibility, and permeability—or how much water can move through a material—are some of the most important physical properties of the materials humans use.

## Metals and Ceramics

Metals are good for building because they're strong and malleable. They are also ductile, meaning they can be pulled into thin wires, and they conduct electricity and heat. Because of these properties, metals are used to move energy within electronic devices and through energy grids. Ceramics, such as porcelain and clay, are strong and waterproof, but they are also brittle. Ceramics are often used for mugs, toilets, bricks, and car brakes.

Ceramic tiles on the floor are smooth to walk on, long-lasting, and easy to clean.

## Plastics and Rubber

Plastics are polymers made from fossil fuels. Plastics may be hard or soft, flexible or stiff, transparent or opaque. They come in many forms and are so versatile that we rely on plastics in nearly every industry.

A rubber band stretches because its molecules are long and tangled. When we pull it, the molecules straighten up and get longer. This stretching is reversible because the molecules eventually return to their old structure.

This boat is made of fiberglass, a material made of a combination of plastic and glass fibers. Fiberglass is strong like glass but also light like plastic.

16

**HALL OF FAME**

Angie Turner King
1905–2004

Angie Turner King's father encouraged her education, and she eventually earned a master's degree in mathematics and chemistry at Cornell University. King had a long career in science education. She taught chemistry to students as well as soldiers during World War II (1939–1945). Many of her students had outstanding careers in science.

Glass or transparent plastic lets sunlight into a greenhouse.

An apron made of waterproof cloth can keep a gardener's clothes dry. A material that doesn't allow water to soak through it is impermeable.

A plastic hose can bend around corners because it's flexible and stretchy.

Plant pots are often made of a stiff, opaque plastic. This holds the dirt in place and keeps too much water from leaking out, allowing the plants to get the water they need.

**DID YOU KNOW?** Diamond is the hardest natural substance on Earth. Diamond-edged tools are even used to drill rocks.

17

# Conductors and Insulators

The properties of conductivity and insulation describe how easily a material lets energy pass through it. This energy can include electricity or thermal energy, also known as heat. Good conductors let energy pass through easily. Good insulators block the flow of energy.

## Thermal Conduction

Heat conduction works because the tiny atoms and molecules that make up solids vibrate with thermal energy. When the material is heated, these particles vibrate faster. Each particle bumps against the particles next to it. This transfers the heat energy to less energetic, or cooler, areas. Most metals are good heat conductors. Plastics, ceramics, and other nonmetals, such as wood, make good insulators.

Stainless steel bottles keep liquids hot or cold. These flasks are metal, but they insulate because there's a vacuum without air between layers of the bottle's walls. This means that heat can't get out of or into the bottle.

The copper pins of an electrical plug connect the wiring in the cable and the wall. The plug and wall socket are made of plastic to protect people from electric shocks.

## Electrical Conduction

Electrical conduction works by allowing a flow of electrons through a material. Metals make good electrical conductors. That's why appliances in our homes use metal wires. These wires are often copper, because this metal is also flexible and ductile.

**DID YOU KNOW?** Polar bear coats have hollow hairs for insulation. Scientists have copied this shape to make carbon tubes with insulating properties.

# Viscosity Oddities

How easily liquids flow is called viscosity. Water runs off surfaces easily because it has low viscosity, but a dollop of honey flows slowly off a spoon. That's because the thick liquid is viscous. Viscous liquids flow slowly because there is friction, or resistance, when the molecules inside them move over one another.

Ketchup is a colloid. It comes out of a bottle more easily if you shake it first. The force of the shaking makes the thick substance act more like a liquid. It gets thinner when forces act on it.

## Viscosity in Newtonian Fluids

Isaac Newton found that the viscosity of normal fluids stays the same as long as temperature stays the same, even when the fluids are pushed or pulled by outside forces. This means that shaking or stirring doesn't change how easily they flow. Fluids like this are Newtonian fluids. Water is a Newtonian fluid. It flows as we expect, whether we sip it from a cup or dive into a swimming pool full of it.

Wiggle your leg out gently if it gets caught in quicksand.

## Non-Newtonian Fluids

Colloids are mixtures with small particles of one substance spread through another substance. They can behave in surprising ways. Someone caught in quicksand, a colloid of sand in water, will float if they relax. However, they will sink if they put force on the quicksand by struggling. Fluids like this, which behave differently when they're disturbed by forces, are called non-Newtonian fluids. Some, such as quicksand, get runnier with forces. Others, including the mixture called Oobleck, get more viscous when force is applied.

**DID YOU KNOW?** When a frog grabs an insect on its tongue, its saliva gets runnier. It flows over the insect and then becomes viscous and sticky again.

**HALL OF FAME**

## Isaac Newton
### 1643–1727

Isaac Newton was a great scientist and mathematician. He explained how forces affect the way objects move with his three laws of motion. But he is best remembered for discovering gravity. He figured out that there are gravitational forces between all objects. One story states that this idea came to him after he saw an apple fall from a tree.

Oobleck is fun non-Newtonian fluid made by mixing cornstarch and water.

Oobleck gets its name from the sticky green substance in a storybook by Dr. Seuss.

Oobleck is a colloid of tiny solid particles dispersed in water. It flows like a liquid, but you can squeeze it into a ball. It gets thicker when forces act on it.

If you poke Oobleck, the particles dispersed in the mixture don't have time to get out of the way of your finger. The force makes the substance act as a solid.

# Changing States

All molecules exist in a certain form called a state of matter. These states are solid, liquid, gas, and plasma. But molecules don't always stay in the same state. For example, when you leave ice out at room temperature, the water changes from a solid to a liquid. In order to change states, the energy of the molecules must change as well.

Dry ice is frozen carbon dioxide. It turns back into gas so quickly that it skips the liquid state. This is called sublimation.

## Physical Change

In a solid, the atoms are held together by strong atomic bonds. These loosen when the solid melts. That's why melting ice loses its shape. The particles in a liquid are held by looser bonds. These loosen more when the liquid evaporates into a gas.

## Temperature

The state of a material is controlled by how much energy its molecules have. Changing a material into a state with more energy requires adding that energy, usually in the form of heat. Gas particles move more than liquid particles, and liquid particles move more than solid particles. So, solids melt and liquids evaporate when they are heated. This heat also weakens the bonds between molecules. When cooled, gases condense into liquids, and liquids freeze.

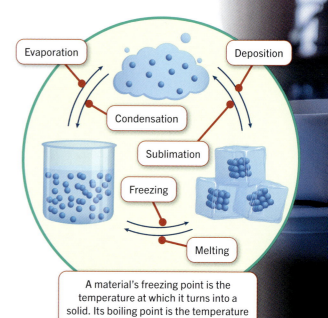

A material's freezing point is the temperature at which it turns into a solid. Its boiling point is the temperature at which it evaporates into a gas.

22 **DID YOU KNOW?** Mercury is the only metal that is liquid at room temperature. It melts at a chilly −37.9 degrees Fahrenheit (−38.8°C).

The steam from a boiling kettle is water vapor escaping into the air.

Packed snow takes longer to absorb heat from the air, so a snow sculpture melts more slowly than snow on the ground.

Cooling water vapor condenses out of the air. It might run down the inside of the kettle.

The large bubbles of gas in a boiling kettle are water evaporating into water vapor.

**HALL OF FAME**

### Maria the Alchemist
### First Century CE

Maria the Alchemist was one of the first early chemists. She was already a historical figure by the fourth century, when Zosimos of Panopolis quoted her work and described her as a sage, or wise person. We think Maria invented some important chemistry tools, including the double boiler for heating things gently. Centuries later, this was given the name bain-marie in her honor.

23

# Mixtures and Solutions

Have you ever made soup from scratch? You have to add many ingredients together to create a whole that looks and tastes different from its separate parts. Creating chemical mixtures or solutions is a similar process. In chemistry, we can add pure substances together to create mixtures, or impure substances.

## Pure and Impure Substances

Chemically pure substances contain only one element, such as gold, or one compound, such as salt. You can't take anything out of a pure substance without changing it chemically. Impure substances are a mixture of elements or compounds. But the elements or compounds in these mixtures are not chemically joined, so they can be easily separated.

Air is a mixture of gases, including oxygen, nitrogen, and carbon dioxide.

This cool, carbonated drink is a mixture of liquid juice, solid ice cubes, and carbon dioxide gas. The carbon dioxide escapes as the fizzy bubbles rise to the top.

## Mixing

If you mix peas into a bowl of water, you can still see the peas. But you can't always see the things in other mixtures. When you stir sugar into tea, the sugar dissolves. This is because the bonds between the sugar molecules break. The sugar seems to disappear, but it is still there. When a solid dissolves into a liquid, it makes a mixture called a solution.

**DID YOU KNOW?** Pure fruit juice has no added sugar, but it's not chemically pure. It contains many compounds.

Salt is soluble because it dissolves in water. Salt is the solute, or the solid that dissolves.

Water is a solvent, meaning it is a substance that other materials can dissolve into.

A salt-water mixture is a solution. Adding more salt makes the solution more concentrated. Adding more water makes it more diluted.

A metal pan is insoluble. It doesn't dissolve in water.

**HALL OF FAME**

### Mary Elliott Hill
### 1907–1969

Mary Elliott Hill was a chemist and teacher who was one of the first Black American women to be awarded a master's degree in chemistry. She encouraged students to study and teach chemistry despite their social difficulties. She and her husband worked together on making soluble compounds used in plastics production.

# Diffusion and Brownian Motion

Solid materials are held in one shape or structure by the bonds between molecules. But in liquids and gases, the molecules are held more weakly together and can move more freely. These movements make the particles diffuse, or spread out evenly. The more energy is added to a substance, the faster and farther apart the molecules diffuse.

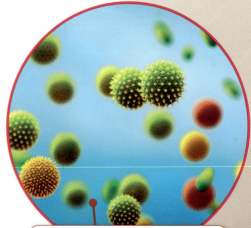

Pollen grains in water will move around randomly. Even though water molecules are much smaller, there are many more of them. So their high-energy movement bumps the pollen around.

## Brownian Motion

Particles in fluids move in all directions at random. This random movement is called Brownian motion. It is named after the botanist Robert Brown, who first observed it in 1827. He looked through a microscope at pollen grains suspended in water and noticed that they moved randomly. Now, we know they were being bumped around by the movements of water molecules that were too small for Brown to see.

**HALL OF FAME**

### Albert Einstein
### 1879–1955

The famous German-born physicist Albert Einstein won the Nobel Prize for his work on electrically charged particles in 1921, but he had many other great ideas. He realized that the movements of pollen grains seen by Robert Brown must be due to collisions with unseen water molecules.

**DID YOU KNOW?** A glass thermometer works because heat makes the liquid inside diffuse and expand, moving up the scale.

## Dissolving and Diffusion

A solid's particles are packed tightly. But when some solids are mixed with a liquid, the bonds holding the solid's particles together are broken. This means that the solid breaks up into small pieces or individual molecules. These molecules diffuse evenly throughout the liquid solvent, and the solid dissolves.

Gas particles have high energy and are fast-moving, so gases diffuse quickly to become evenly spread out.

When a dye is splashed into water, the particles are close together at first. There is a high concentration of color in one area and a low concentration everywhere else.

The particles of both liquids move at random and bump into each other. This spreads the particles and mixes them up.

The dye and water particles diffuse through each other until they are evenly mixed. Eventually, there will be an even concentration of color and water particles all throughout the solution.

# Separating Solids from Mixtures

Whether pouring sugar into a drink or mixing concrete, people mix substances together all the time. It's an easy way to create new and useful substances. But it is much harder to unmix these chemicals once they are combined. The best method for separating a mixture depends on which substances are mixed together.

## Sieving and Filtering

Different-sized solids can be separated by sieving. The holes in the mesh of a sieve let small objects pass through but stop anything bigger. A filter is like a sieve and is used to separate pieces of solids from liquids or gases. Straining boiling water and pasta in a colander and passing water and coffee grounds through a filter are both forms of filtering.

## Evaporation

We can separate a dissolved solid from a solvent through evaporation. The liquid is heated until it turns into a gas, and the pure solid is left behind. The amount of the solid stays the same.

Traditional sea salt farmers let seawater evaporate in shallow pools. The salt crystals left behind are harvested.

**HALL OF FAME**

### Charles Richard Drew
### 1904–1950

Charles Richard Drew was a Black American surgeon who studied blood chemistry. He discovered that donated blood lasted longer if the red blood cells were separated from the rest of the blood. His work on improved blood storage saved many lives during World War II, and he is known as the father of the blood bank.

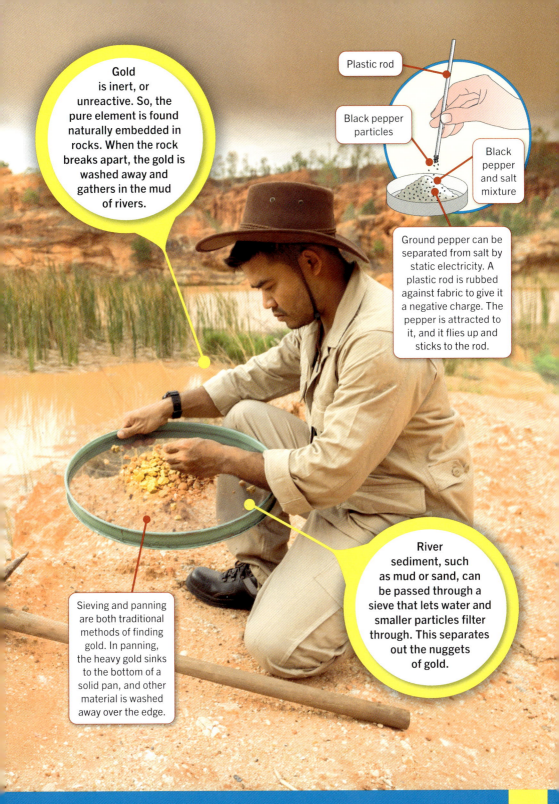

# Separating Solutions

Separating the substances in a solution can take a few steps. Heating a solution until one liquid evaporates can take one substance out of the solution. The evaporated part can then be collected by turning it back into a liquid. This process is called distillation.

## Simple Distillation

Separating a liquid out of a solution requires simple distillation. This purifies the liquid by removing the other substance. To collect pure water from a salt and water solution, the solution is heated until it boils. The water component evaporates, leaving behind the salt crystals. The water vapor is cooled and collected.

## Fractional Distillation

Some solutions contain several different liquid components, or fractions. The different fractions can be separated out and collected by fractional distillation. This process works because different liquids boil at different temperatures. They evaporate at different times during heating, so their vapors can be collected separately. Fractional distillation is used in oil refineries to separate crude oil into a range of fuels and compounds that are used in many industries.

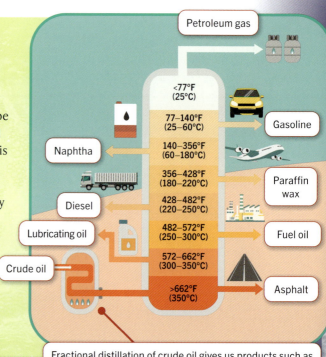

Fractional distillation of crude oil gives us products such as asphalt for road surfaces and gasoline for cars. Different fractions are used in various manufacturing industries.

**HALL OF FAME**

**Alice Augusta Ball**
**1892–1916**

Alice Augusta Ball studied seed oils from the chaulmoogra tree to treat the infectious Hansen's disease. She separated the oils by fractionation, which made the active ingredients more soluble. The new and improved medicine could be injected, and this meant that patients were able to interact with the general population once they were treated.

The mixture is heated until the temperature reaches the boiling point of the first liquid. This liquid turns into a vapor.

The hot vapor flows through the condenser. This has a jacket of cold water flowing around it.

The vapor is cooled by the condenser and turns back into a liquid.

Distillation can be used to separate a liquid that boils at a low temperature from a mixture of liquids.

The pure liquid collects in a beaker.

**DID YOU KNOW?** Oil refineries heat crude oil in fractionating towers. The world's tallest fractionating tower is in Nigeria and is 369 feet (112 m) high!

# Reactions

When substances react, the resulting products have new properties. The atoms of the reactants rearrange as their bonds break and new bonds form. No atoms are lost, so the same atoms are combined, albeit differently, in the reactants as were present in the products.

## Chemical Equations

Chemists use equations to describe what happens in a reaction. A chemical equation uses chemical symbols and formulas to show the type and number of atoms in the molecules of the reactants and products. For example, the equation for the reaction of carbon and oxygen to make carbon dioxide is $C + O_2 \longrightarrow CO_2$. This equation shows that one atom of carbon reacts with two atoms of oxygen to make a carbon dioxide molecule containing one carbon and two oxygen atoms. The equation is balanced, with three atoms before the arrow and three atoms after it.

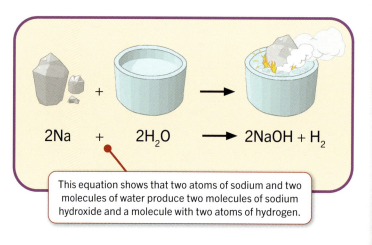

$2Na + 2H_2O \longrightarrow 2NaOH + H_2$

This equation shows that two atoms of sodium and two molecules of water produce two molecules of sodium hydroxide and a molecule with two atoms of hydrogen.

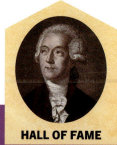

**Antoine Lavoisier**
1743–1794

Antoine Lavoisier developed a theory of chemical reactivity that showed that the same amount of matter exists after a reaction as before. In 1789, he published a book stating this theory for the first time. The book also introduced a new way of naming compounds that is still the basis of chemical names today.

**HALL OF FAME**

## Reactivity

Reactivity is how readily a chemical reacts with others. Some metals, such as sodium, are so reactive that they are found only as compounds in nature. Others, such as gold, are not reactive at all. Sodium is more reactive than copper, which is more reactive than silver, which is more reactive than gold. A more reactive metal will replace a less reactive metal in a compound in solution. This is called displacement.

When copper wire is suspended in a clear silver nitrate solution, copper atoms take the place of silver and change the solution to blue copper nitrate. The displaced silver forms crystals on the wire.

Atoms bond like a group of dancers holding hands. They can bond together, and then they can let go, move around, and find new partners.

The members of the group stay the same, even when they move around or change partners.

**DID YOU KNOW?** Chemical reactions keep us alive. Trillions of biochemical reactions are happening in your body right now.

33

# Radioactivity

Each element has its own number of protons in its nucleus. But the number of neutrons is different in different isotopes, or forms, of an element. An isotope with more neutrons than usual is unstable and decays, giving off energy as radioactive particles and rays until it transforms into a more stable isotope or even a different element. This is a reaction called radioactivity.

Radioactivity disturbs the electrons of a gas in an instrument called a Geiger counter, helping people know when there is dangerous radiation nearby.

## Half-life

When unstable isotopes—sometimes called radioisotopes—decay, their nuclei give off three types of radiation. The first is an alpha particle made of two protons and two neutrons. The second is beta radiation, which is when an atom sends out an electron. The third, gamma radiation, is a form of electromagnetic energy that moves in waves. This reaction changes the number of subatomic particles, which means that radioactive elements change into other elements. This radioactive decay occurs atom by atom, and it happens at different rates for different radioisotopes. A radioactive isotope's half-life is the time it takes for half of its nucleus to decay into the atoms of another element.

The age of pigments in prehistoric cave paintings can be found using carbon dating. Carbon-14 can date objects up to 60,000 years old.

### Carbon Dating

Free neutrons that are not held in an atomic nucleus occur high in the atmosphere. When one bumps into a nitrogen atom in the air, the nitrogen gains a neutron and releases a proton. This changes the nitrogen into an atom of carbon-14. Carbon-14 atoms become part of carbon dioxide molecules and enter the food chain through plants. Carbon-14 is weakly radioactive. All living things contain a known percentage of it. When they die, those carbon-14 atoms decay slowly back into nitrogen. The half-life is 5,700 years. Scientists measure the amount of carbon-14 in organic matter to determine how old things are. This is called carbon dating.

**DID YOU KNOW?** Earth's background radiation causes changes to the genes inside of cells. These changes drive natural evolution.

Paper or skin · Lead · Aluminum · Concrete

α alpha
β beta
γ gamma
n neutron

Different types of radiation travel farther and are blocked by different materials.

Nuclear radiation can harm living cells, so it can also be helpful in killing germs, such as those on food and medical equipment, or killing damaged cells in cancer patients.

In nuclear fission reactors, neutrons bombard the isotopes of heavy elements to split the nuclei. A chain reaction releases more neutrons as well as a lot of energy, which is used to make electricity.

A neutron can break up into a positive proton and a negative electron. The electrons released in beta radiation come from the nucleus, not from the energy shells of the atom.

### Henri Becquerel
### 1852–1908

French physicist Henri Becquerel was looking for X-rays in fluorescent materials when he accidentally discovered radioactivity instead. He found that tiny bits of uranium sulfate left afterimages on photographic film. He received the Nobel Prize in Physics in 1903 jointly with Marie and Pierre Curie, and the becquerel unit of radioactivity was named after him.

**HALL OF FAME**

# Reversible and Irreversible Changes

In a chemical reaction, the reactants' atoms rearrange to make the products. Some reactions are reversible. For example, nitrogen dioxide gas breaks down into nitrogen monoxide and oxygen when heated, and then it changes back when cooled. Other reactions, such as burning and corrosion, are irreversible. It's impossible to get the original reactants back.

## Cooking and Combustion

A cook can't unbake a cake because the ingredients have been permanently, chemically changed. Baking a cake involves reactions such as thermal decomposition, which is breaking apart a substance by heat. Combustion, the process of a fuel burning in air, is another useful but irreversible reaction. A fuel, such as wood, reacts with oxygen in the air to release energy in the form of light and heat. But we can't turn the ash back into wood.

Color can neatly demonstrate a reversible change. A flask of nitrogen dioxide loses its color when heated, and it returns to red-brown when cooled.

**HALL OF FAME**

### William Jacob Knox
### 1904–1995

William Jacob Knox earned a doctorate in chemistry at the Massachusetts Institute of Technology. During World War II, he was a supervisor in the Manhattan Project, using the corrosive gas uranium hexafluoride to separate isotopes. Later, he became the second Black chemist ever to work at the Eastman Kodak company. The lifelong racial prejudice he faced inspired him to fight for civil rights, and he set up scholarships to help minority students.

**DID YOU KNOW?** The planet Mars is rusty red because iron in its soil reacted with oxygen billions of years ago.

## Corrosion and rusting

Corrosion is a reaction in which a metal oxidizes. That means it gains oxygen from the air and changes into a type of chemical called a metal oxide. This is an example of an irreversible change and can be a problem in buildings. The metal gets weaker as it continues to gain oxygen and corrode. Rusting is the type of corrosion that happens when iron is exposed to oxygen in air or water.

Iron reacts with oxygen to produce iron oxide, or rust.

The Statue of Liberty is made of iron covered with copper sheets. Copper reacts with oxygen in the air to form copper oxide.

The copper oxide has reacted with carbon dioxide, sulfur, and salt in the air to create the copper compounds that make the blue-green pigment called verdigris.

The Statue of Liberty with its pedestal is 305 ft. (93 m) tall. It has stood on Liberty Island since 1886. The blue-green statue was once a bright red-brown, similar to the color of a new copper penny.

The verdigris keeps the copper underneath from reacting more, so the statue is protected by the corrosion on the surface.

37

# Exothermic and Endothermic Reactions

As bonds are broken during a chemical reaction, energy is taken in. Energy is released as bonds reform. The difference in the energy absorbed and released by all the bonds makes the total reaction either endothermic or exothermic—the reaction either absorbs or releases energy, usually in the form of heat.

Nitric acid is a strong oxidizing chemical, meaning it provides oxygen for reactions, and it can produce violent exothermic reactions in the form of explosions.

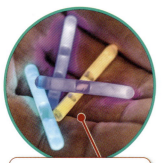

When you snap a glow stick, you start an exothermic reaction that releases energy in the form of light.

## Exothermic Reactions

Exothermic reactions release energy overall, so they often give off heat. Many oxidation reactions are exothermic. Disposable hand warmers use a surprising exothermic oxidation reaction— rusting! These pouches contain separated water and iron powder. When they are activated, the iron reacts with oxygen in the water, producing iron oxide, or rust, as well as heat. Respiration, or breathing, is another exothermic reaction. It uses oxygen to produce energy for your body to use.

**HALL OF FAME**

**May Sybil Leslie**
**1887–1937**

May Sybil Leslie perfected the manufacturing conditions for nitric acid, which is used in explosives production, in a government laboratory during World War I (1914–1918). She was an English chemist who worked for a time with the Nobel Prize winner Marie Curie and studied the radioactive compounds of thorium and actinium. She was only 49 when she died, possibly due to radiation exposure.

## Endothermic Reactions

In endothermic reactions, more energy is absorbed than released. So these reactions can cool their surroundings. Cooking and thermal decomposition are endothermic. A cake mixture needs to absorb heat so that the ingredients can turn into a cake. Photosynthesis, in which plants turn carbon dioxide and water into glucose and oxygen, is also endothermic. Plants absorb the sun's energy to fuel the reaction.

The thermal decomposition of sodium bicarbonate, or baking soda, in a cake means that the baking powder breaks down to produce carbon dioxide. This makes the batter rise.

Combustion is an example of an exothermic reaction. It releases lots of energy in the form of heat and light.

As well as energy, the products of combustion are carbon dioxide and water. Bonfire smoke also contains carbon monoxide and other chemical products of the reaction.

This fire will burn until all the fuel has been used up and only ash is left.

We ignite a bonfire with a source of heat, such as a match. Then, we enjoy the warmth of the fire as the fuel burns.

**DID YOU KNOW?** Australian brush turkeys don't sit on their eggs; they build a compost pile on them that keeps them warm. This works because composting is exothermic.

# Speeding Up Reactions

Atoms and molecules react when they collide if they carry enough energy to break their bonds. Increasing either the number of collisions or the energy of the particles speeds up a chemical reaction. You can do this by raising the temperature or pressure or by adding more reactant so that there are more particles to collide.

Enzymes are biological catalysts that speed up biochemical reactions in living organisms. The enzymes in yeast, a fungus, help bread rise.

## Magical Catalysts

Catalysts speed up reactions. They don't change the products of the reaction, and they aren't changed themselves, so they can be used again and again. They make reactions happen faster, so more of a product can be made in less time. They also make reactions happen at lower temperatures. Only a very small amount of catalyst is needed to improve a reaction. This all makes catalysts very useful in manufacturing industries.

## The Secret of Catalysts

Catalysts work by letting a reaction happen at a lower activation energy. They don't increase the number of collisions, but they make more of the collisions that cause bonds to break. Not all reactions have a suitable catalyst, and different catalysts work for different processes. For example, zinc oxide speeds up the reaction of methane and oxygen to make methanol, which is used to make many more chemicals.

Catalytic converters contain rhodium and platinum catalysts. They force harmful car engine gases, such as nitrogen oxides and carbon monoxide, to react together to produce less harmful gases.

**DID YOU KNOW?** Scientists are using computers to develop new catalysts that may revolutionize electric car batteries.

**HALL OF FAME**

**Edith Flanigen**
**born 1929**

Edith Flanigen is an American chemist and inventor of molecular sieves, natural and synthetic materials used as filters and catalysts in industry. Among the materials she developed is zeolite Y, used to break down crude oil and make oil refining cleaner and safer. Flanigen received many awards and patents for her work in cleaner fuels and environmental cleanup. She was awarded the National Medal of Technology and Innovation in 2014.

Margarine is made from vegetable oils that contain some double bonds. These molecules are unsaturated.

A zeolite catalyst makes a molecular sieve that can trap molecules and separate them by size. Zeolite crystals are the coating on this wire mesh.

Hydrogenation raises the melting point of margarine, so it is solid at room temperature.

In hydrogenation, hydrogen atoms join up with oil molecules so the double bonds become single bonds. Manufacturers use nickel as a catalyst to speed up the hydrogenation process.

41

# Molecules Make the World

From digesting food to creating energy from nuclear power, our lives would not be possible without molecular reactions. Every year, chemists are learning more about existing molecules and even creating new ones by experimenting with chemical reactions. By studying the properties of these molecules, scientists are uncovering age-old mysteries and inventing new technologies.

## Cancer-Fighting Molecules

Recently, scientists have been studying how cancers use proteins to spread. They have discovered molecules that interfere with these proteins, allowing antibodies to attach to cancer cells. This helps mark cancer cells as targets for the immune system, making it easier for a person's body to fight cancer.

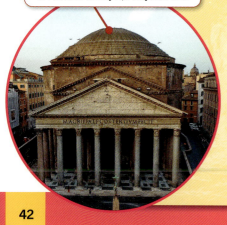

The concrete dome of the Pantheon in Rome is nearly 2,000 years old.

## Ancient Concrete

Experts have long wondered how ancient Romans made concrete that lasted thousands of years. Modern chemists think they have discovered the answer. Romans likely mixed volcanic ash, quicklime, and water. This created a reaction that left lumps of quicklime within the mixture. As rain hits this concrete, the quicklime reacts and creates tiny crystals that fill in cracks and strengthen the structure.

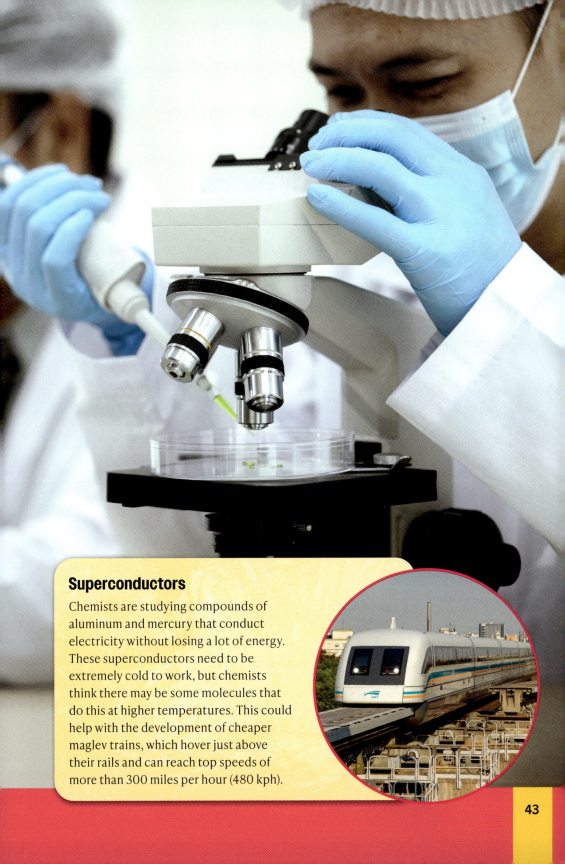

## Superconductors

Chemists are studying compounds of aluminum and mercury that conduct electricity without losing a lot of energy. These superconductors need to be extremely cold to work, but chemists think there may be some molecules that do this at higher temperatures. This could help with the development of cheaper maglev trains, which hover just above their rails and can reach top speeds of more than 300 miles per hour (480 kph).

# Review and Reflect

Now that you've read about molecules and chemical reactions, let's review what you've learned. Use the following questions to reflect on your newfound knowledge and integrate it with what you already knew.

## Check for Understanding

1. What force holds an atom together? *(p. 6)*

2. Which two elements are liquids at room temperature? *(p. 8)*

3. What does it mean when an element is stable? *(p. 10)*

4. How does a diatomic molecule form? What does it mean when a molecule is homonuclear? *(p. 12)*

5. What elements make up the chemical $H_2O$? *(p. 14)*

6. What makes a good conductor? What makes a good insulator? *(p. 18)*

7. Define what a colloid is and list three examples. *(pp. 20-21)*

8. Name three ways a material can change states of matter. *(pp. 22-23)*

9. What is the difference between pure and impure substances? *(p. 24)*

10. Describe Brownian motion and how it was first observed. *(p. 26)*

11. When would you use a sieve? When would you use a filter? *(p. 28)*

12. Explain how simple distillation works. *(p. 30)*

13. Name one example of an irreversible change. *(pp. 36-37)*

14. What is the difference between an exothermic and an endothermic reaction? List an example of each. *(pp. 38-39)*

15. How does a catalyst work? *(p. 40)*

44

## Making Connections

1. Explain how the number of electrons an atom has and how they are arranged affects the reactivity of an element.

2. What role does temperature play in changing states of matter? List three examples of reactions in which changing temperature is a crucial factor.

3. Describe the relationship between a solute and a solvent.

4. Choose two of the following methods of separating matter to compare and contrast: sieving, filtering, evaporation, and distillation.

5. What is one way in which cooking and chemistry are similar?

## In Your Own Words

1. Choose a person from one of the Hall of Fame sidebars and explain how their discoveries impacted the world.

2. There are many ways to combine and separate matter. Think of two substances that can be combined, and then explain if they can be separated. If so, explain how using one of the methods described in this book could help separate these chemicals.

3. Which concept in this book interested you the most? What are some methods you could use to learn more?

4. Imagine if chemists had never figured out how to combine substances to make new materials. In what ways do you think your life would be different?

5. There are many ways to tell if a chemical reaction has occurred. What are some of the indicators shown in this book? Are there any indicators you can think of that weren't in this book?

# Glossary

**acid** a chemical with a value lower than 7 on the pH scale

**alkali** a chemical with a value higher than 7 on the pH scale

**atom** the smallest unit of a chemical element

**atomic number** the number of protons in an atom

**chemical reaction** a process in which atoms are rearranged, changing one or more substances into different substances

**compound** a pure chemical made from the atoms of more than one element

**conductor** a material that lets heat or electricity pass through it

**crystal** a solid material in which the particles are joined together in a repeating pattern

**density** the space a substance takes up in relation to the amount of matter in the substance

**dissolve** to mix a solid into a liquid until the solid is no longer visible

**distillation** a process by which a mixture made up of liquids with different boiling points can be separated

**electron** a negatively charged particle found in an atom

**element** a chemical made of a single type of atom

**filtering** separating solid particles from a fluid

**formula** the way scientists write down symbols to show the number and type of atoms present in a molecule

**fossil fuels** nonrenewable energy sources such as coal, crude oil, and natural gas

**insulator** a material that heat or electricity cannot pass through

**isotopes** forms of an element with different numbers of neutrons

**molecule** a group of two or more atoms that are chemically bonded

**oxidation** a reaction in which a chemical gains oxygen atoms

**radioactive** giving off energy in the form of small particles or waves

**reactivity** a measure of how easily a substance reacts with other substances

**soluble** the ability to dissolve in liquids such as water

**solution** a mixture in which something has been dissolved within a liquid

46

## Read More

**Dingle, Adrian.** *My Book of the Elements (My Book).* New York: DK Publishing, 2024.

**Faust, Daniel R.** *Chemical Reactions (Intro to Chemistry).* Minneapolis: Bearport Publishing Company, 2023.

**McKenzie, Precious.** *The Micro World of Atoms and Molecules (Micro Science).* North Mankato, MN: Capstone Press, 2022.

**O'Daly, Anne.** *The Basics of Chemical Reactions (Core Concepts).* New York: Rosen Publishing, 2024.

## Learn More Online

1. Go to **FactSurfer.com** or scan the QR code below.
2. Enter "**Molecules Chemical Reactions**" into the search box.
3. Click on the cover of this book to see a list of websites.

# Index

acids  4
alkalis  10–11
atomic numbers  6, 8, 10
batteries  10, 40
Brownian motion  26
carbon dating  34
catalysts  40–41
ceramics  18
combustion  39
condensation  22
conduction  18
convection  19
crude oil  30–31, 41
crystals  12, 28, 30, 33, 41–42
diffusion  26
distillation  30
DNA  13
electricity  7, 9, 16, 18–19, 29, 35, 43
energy shells  6, 10–12, 35
evaporation  28
explosions  4, 38
fertilizers  10
filtering  28
fireworks  4, 10
fluids  19–20, 26
food  19, 29, 34–35, 42
fossil fuels  16
fractional distillation  30
gasoline  30

glucose  39
gold  8–9, 24, 29, 33
graphite  12–13
insulators  18–19
medicines  31
metals  8, 10–11, 16, 18–19, 33
Oobleck  20–21
petroleum  30
photosynthesis  39
plastics  16, 25
polymers  16
radioactivity  34–35
rocks  8, 17, 29
rubber  16
salt  11, 14, 24–25, 28–30, 37
sieving  28
soil  36
solutions  24, 30
solvents  25, 28
temperature  8, 20, 22, 31, 40–41
thermal energy  18
thermometers  26
viscosity  20
X-rays  35